ACTION-ADVENTURE GAMES

By

Kirsty Holmes

BookLife
PUBLISHING

©2019
BookLife Publishing Ltd.
King's Lynn
Norfolk PE30 4LS
All rights reserved.
Printed in Malaysia.

A catalogue record for this book is available from the British Library.

ISBN: 9781-78637-528-5

Written by:
Kirsty Holmes

Edited by:
Holly Duhig

Designed by:
Gareth Liddington

CONTENTS

Words that look like *this* can be accessed
in the <<GLOSSARY>> on page 31

WELCOME TO THE ARCADE

Ever since the very first adventuring archaeologist (say: ark-ee-ollo-gist) pushed open the first tomb, or the first space hero fired up the warp drive, fearless kids like you and me have been swinging into the action, pistols at the ready. Does the thought of treasure hunting make you feel scared – or excited? If you are grabbing your backpack and heading for the chopper right now, you're in the right place! We're going to head for the Arcade, check the historical records, and dodge the lasers all the way to the end. This gaming guide will let you build your skills, taking you from small fry to big fish in the world of action-adventure games. So, what are you waiting for – GET YOUR GAME ON!

Woooooo hoooooooo! Hey! Look out! We've got to get into the Arcade before the killer wasps get us! Mind the spikes – and the fire! Duck! Oh, we made it! Phew! Hey, fellow adventurer! My real name is Pixelle, and I'm an action hero! Want to come with me on an adventure?

Let's start with the basics. A video game is an *electronic* game that needs a player (that's you) to use a device (that's the thing you play on) to make stuff happen on a screen. Usually that screen is a television or a computer monitor, but you can play games on mobile phones, hand-held gaming devices, or tablets too. To play on your television you will need a console – this is a special type of computer just for playing video games. If you play on a computer screen you will probably use a PC. This stands for personal computer and is a type of computer designed to be used at home by regular people for lots of things – like doing homework or using the internet – and playing games, of course! There are lots of types of video games – from *pixel*-perfect platformers and puzzlers to amazing action-adventure games that will see you virtually risking virtual life and limb: there is something for everyone in a video game.

Light guns armed? Check. Sandwiches packed? Check. Danger round every corner? DOUBLE CHECK! I hear the wasps right behind us – but luckily, I know a shortcut! Quick! Into the Arcade! Follow me!

<<Player One... Ready...?>>

ARCADE

DATA FILE: ACTION-ADVENTURE GAMES

Action-adventure games are games where it's all about the action… and the adventure! Players usually play as one main character, who will go on a journey or adventure. There will be lots of climbing, jumping, shooting, fighting and running for your life! Depending on the type of game, you will need different skills. Some games are all about precision jumping and *parkour*-like climbing. Others are about strength and bravery, or puzzle-solving. But they all have one thing in common: it won't be a walk in the park! The main story or adventure is called the main quest. In many games there are also *side quests*: small, *fetch quests* or bonus puzzles, which can earn you bonuses. Most main storylines are played by a single player, but games exist where working co-operatively, or within online arenas is the only way to win, . Games vary in difficulty and how complicated they are. Action-adventure games can be played on just about every *platform*, from consoles to mobile phones.

Arcade — we're ready to start. Load data.

<<LOADING… DATA LEVEL ONE: WHAT IS AN ACTION-ADVENTURE GAME>>

OBJECTIVE
● Slay Golem (0/1)

PLAYER HEALTH

INVENTORY

ENEMY HEALTH

RADAR

RETICLE

SUBTITLES

"There it is! Take down the Golem and report back to camp!"

ACTION-ADVENTURE

Action-Adventure is one of the vaguest terms when describing games, but generally it suggests a mix of **combat**, puzzle-solving, and general exploration.

ACTION

Strictly speaking, this is a separate **genre**. An action game is almost completely focused on combat of some kind, with the action coming thick and fast, often with huge **boss fights**.

ADVENTURE

Adventure games are usually not violent, and more focussed on the story. This genre includes point-and-click adventures, text adventures, and interactive **first-person** games.

RPG

Role-playing games allow the player to take on a character or role, in order to complete the game. Character and storyline are very important in these games.

SIDE-SCROLLING

Some games that are technically 2D platform games have an emphasis on puzzle solving, combat, and exploration; exactly like action-adventure games.

METROIDVANIA

Exploration based games (such as Metroid and Castlevania) started in 2D, but modern games increasingly have players unlocking new areas and changing the way they explore when they get new abilities.

<<KILLER BYTES>>
- POINT-AND-CLICK = CLICK ITEMS ON A SCREEN TO FIGURE OUT CLUES
- TEXT ADVENTURE = NO PICTURES; THE STORY IS TOLD IN WRITING

FACT FILE: LEGO

If you like LEGO as much as you like video games, then you probably know all about the games we're going to look at next. The LEGO series has been ongoing for more than a *decade*, with the first games landing all the way back in 2006. The one that really got the ball rolling was LEGO Star Wars: The Original Trilogy, which was followed the next year with even more blocky Star Wars goodness before Batman got the LEGO treatment too.

Since then we've been getting one or two (or even more) LEGO games every year, from comic giants DC and Marvel to Harry Potter and Jurassic World and even a bunch of LEGO's own *franchises* like LEGO City and Ninjago. Regardless of the series, the games all have a few things in common; the most obvious traits being that you control LEGO characters, and use their special skills to solve puzzles and take out bad guys.

Over the years, the games have become more and more complicated, with developer TT Games – the TT stands for Traveller's Tales – building on each new entry with fresh features and different ideas. We've seen new ways to build with blocks in-game, we've seen open worlds, crazy new abilities, the addition of voice acting, and improved combat mechanics. More recently we even got a *toys-to-life* platform called LEGO Dimensions, which let players place LEGO mini-figures on a real-world portal so they then appear on the screen.

LEGO games are everywhere, from consoles to mobiles and everything in-between. They're nearly all action-adventure games that involve puzzle-solving, a bit of platforming, and engaging in combat with a range of different enemy types. With new series and features being added every year, there's no chance of this gaming *phenomenon* going away any time soon.

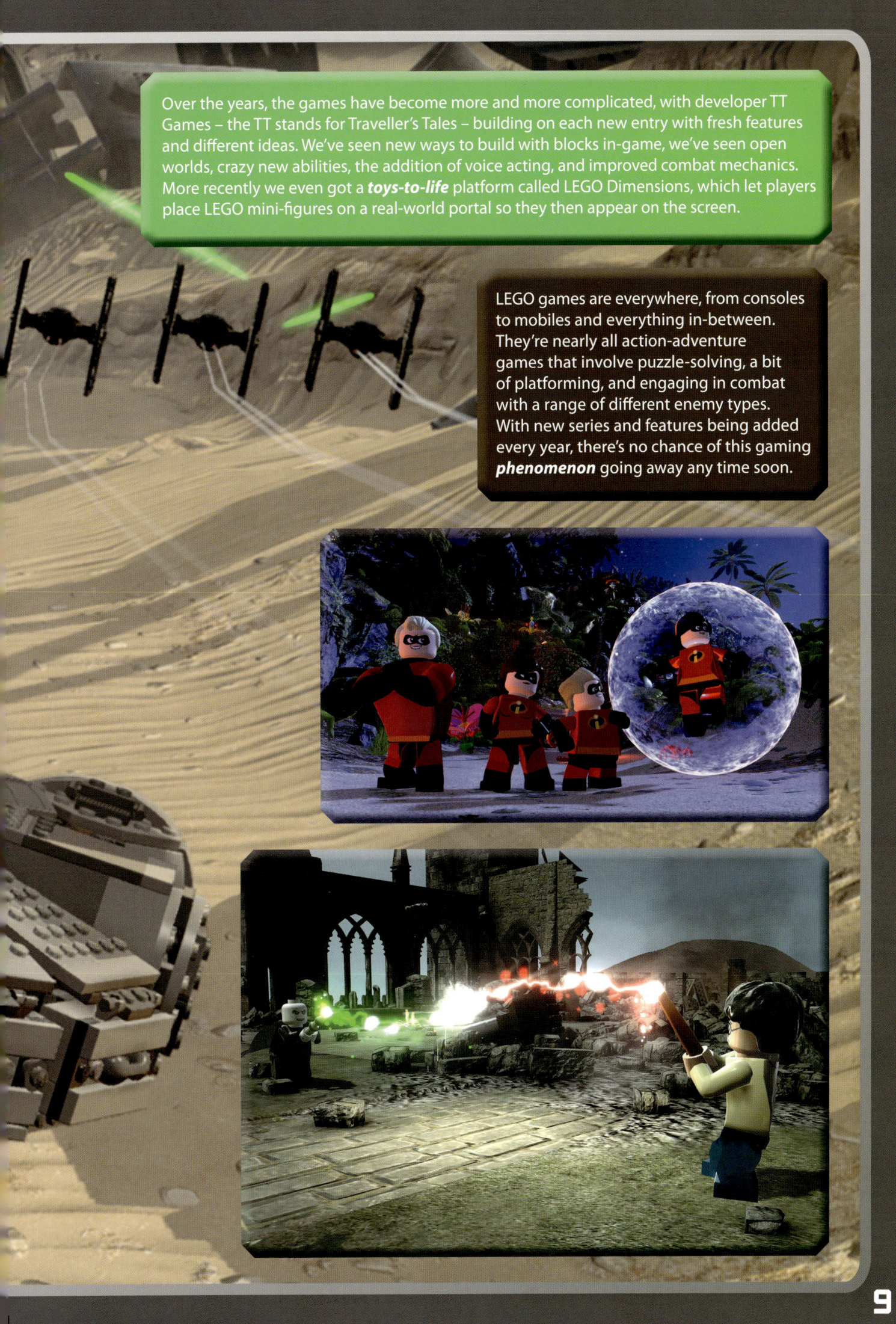

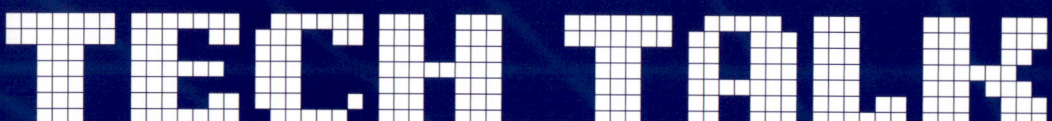

TECH TALK

If you're going to get ahead in action-adventure games, you need to know what you're talking about. This data file will give you what you need to know to get in on the action and have an adventure. Arcade, quick! Tell us what we need to know before the bees come!

<<LOADING... DATA LEVEL THREE: WHAT YOU NEED TO KNOW>>

PLAYER INFO

Usually, action-adventure games are single-player. Your hero could have a whole team of *AI*-based sidekicks, but you're in charge. Many games also have online multiplayer or arena modes where you can test your skills in challenges, often with friends.

PERIPHERALS

(say: per-if-er-als) are things you plug into the console or PC to play the game. Most action games just need a controller, or a keyboard if you play on PC.

VISUALS

Action-adventure games are usually shown in the third-person, where the player is looking at their character from the outside. A few games may use a first-person viewpoint, as if you are looking out of the character's eyes.

OBJECTIVES

Most games have a clear *objective*: rescue someone, fetch something, or save somewhere from destruction. The main quest will be focused on this objective. Depending on how complex the game is, you might have side quests to complete too.

LEVELS

These games don't usually have clear, numbered levels. Instead, they have something called scaling difficulty. This means that, as you get better at defeating basic enemies, more and more challenging enemies start to appear. Early stages of the game will teach simple skills, often presented as part of the story. As you progress, you learn new skills to meet new challenges.

FACT FILE:
THE LEGEND OF ZELDA

Let's start with The Legend of Zelda: Breath of the Wild and work our way back. The latest game in Nintendo's series was released alongside the company's latest console, the Switch, and appeared on the new handheld home console and its predecessor, the Wii U.

Breath of the Wild was the biggest and most ambitious Zelda game to date. Our long-time hero, Link, wakes up after a very long sleep and finds that the land of Hyrule is very different to how he left it, and embarks on a mission to free the land from Calamity Ganon. And so begins an epic journey across the kingdom where Link must battle monsters, help the locals, explore puzzling shrines, and climb up to hard-to-reach places.

The Zelda games have always been a bit cleverer than your average dungeon-crawling adventure, and there's a puzzle element present throughout nearly all of the games in the series. In Breath of the Wild this was taken to another level with both challenging shrines to discover and conquer, but also in-game physics that require the player to think about their surroundings. Heading up to the ice-covered mountains? You'll freeze if you go up there without making plans, so Link will either need to wrap up warm, build a fire, or make and take a potion to keep him warm while he explores the colder parts of the world.

The Legend of Zelda series has grown up with Nintendo's consoles. The series started out as *top-down* action-adventures on the old NES and SNES systems, before going 3D on the N64 with *iconic* games such as Ocarina of Time and Majora's Mask. Since then, we've seen motion-controlled sword fights, handheld co-op adventures, and now open-world exploration. Nintendo's fantasy series is one the most iconic in gaming for a reason. When it comes to thoughtful game design, Link and friends are one step ahead of the competition.

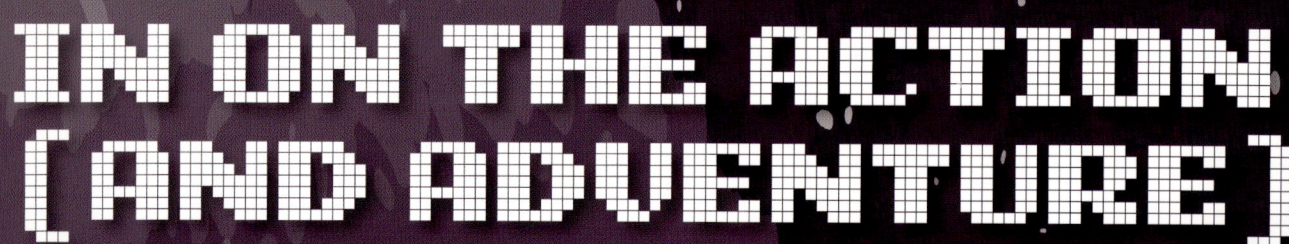

IN ON THE ACTION (AND ADVENTURE)

In action-adventure games, you're going to need to use every skill, clue, and fragment of knowledge that you have if you're going to survive. Write these survival tips in your journal. You're going to need them...

SKILLS

Because they are so *diverse*, each action-adventure game will require different skills, but for all action-adventure games, you will need a few different tricks up your sleeve.

PUZZLE-SOLVING

- Try, try and try again
- Stop and think – and make notes
- Look for patterns and groups
- Check your inventory and notes
- Work backwards

QUICK-TIME EVENTS

- Look for button icons on screen
- React quickly – you'll run out of time
- If you don't act, the computer will choose

JUMPING & CLIMBING

- Look before you leap!
- Look for ropes, ladders and vines
- Use both short and long jumps
- Look for window ledges and other handholds
- Characters will sometimes reach if it's safe to jump

ATTACK AND DEFENCE

- Learn how to fight properly – don't just button-bash
- Learn how to defend and block attacks
- Learn how to use cover
- Keep an eye on your health
- Check your surroundings

PLAYER SKILLS

- Quick reflexes – you need to act fast!
- Concentration – stay alert and remember facts
- Hang in there – be willing to *persevere*
- Think outside the box – look for lots of ways to solve a problem
- Memory – remember clues, names and numbers

INVENTORY
THINGS YOU'LL FIND ALONG THE WAY

CLUES

Little white paint streaks showing you where to climb? A glowing trail leading through the woods? Suddenly surrounded by enemies? Is that chest FULL of health potions? Chances are, you're going the right way.

STORYLINE

From once upon a time in space to happily ever after under the sea. Most games have huge, sweeping storylines, taking you to far-off lands to achieve your goals. You'll bump into a lot of 'Chosen Ones' in this genre.

MAP MARKERS

Use your map to work out where you are and where you need to go. If you have a compass on-screen it might show you your destination, and incoming enemies or allies.

COLLECTIBLES

Fill your backpack with important items: weapons, health packs or potions, quest items, map pieces, the occasional life-saving cabbage…

COMPANIONS

Meet new people and make new friends – and some may join you along the way. AI-controlled companion characters can bring new abilities to a group, or you might gain a doggy friend to help you in fights and keep you company.

FACT FILE: TOMB RAIDER

Tomb Raider might be a popular series, but it's leading lady Lara Croft who steals the show. Ms Croft's first adventure, which launched back in 1996, kick-started the career of a genuine gaming icon. The violent adventurer took her British brand of exploration and puzzle-solving to all corners of the world in search of hidden treasure. The games were great, sure, but it was Lara who stole the show and turned the series into a household name.

The games have been worked on by different studios in different countries, there have been puzzle-driven adventures, open-world action games, mobile puzzle titles, and even twin-stick shooters, but the thing that links them all is Ms Croft.

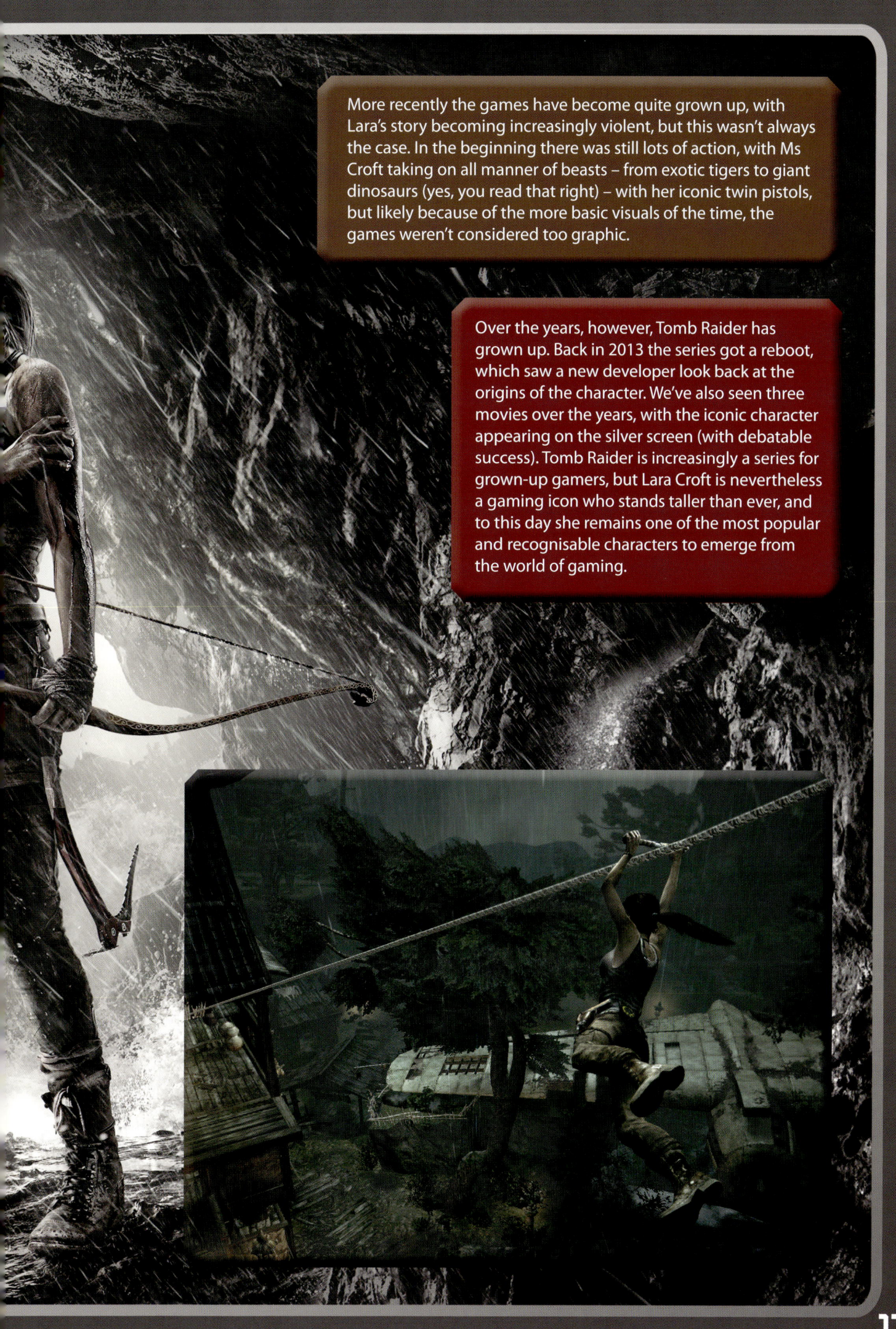

More recently the games have become quite grown up, with Lara's story becoming increasingly violent, but this wasn't always the case. In the beginning there was still lots of action, with Ms Croft taking on all manner of beasts – from exotic tigers to giant dinosaurs (yes, you read that right) – with her iconic twin pistols, but likely because of the more basic visuals of the time, the games weren't considered too graphic.

Over the years, however, Tomb Raider has grown up. Back in 2013 the series got a reboot, which saw a new developer look back at the origins of the character. We've also seen three movies over the years, with the iconic character appearing on the silver screen (with debatable success). Tomb Raider is increasingly a series for grown-up gamers, but Lara Croft is nevertheless a gaming icon who stands taller than ever, and to this day she remains one of the most popular and recognisable characters to emerge from the world of gaming.

GET YOUR GAME ON

Phew! Let's take a moment to regroup. We need a clear path through this game and out the other side of the Arcade. Let's load up the how-to guide and see how far through the game we are.

<<LOADING... DATA LEVEL FOUR: HOW TO PLAY>>

FIND YOUR FEET

Nowadays, games are very clever at teaching us how to play them. Instead of a list of instructions, now you might find yourself starting in the middle of the action, and on-screen prompts will teach you the controls at the same time as showing you who and where you are. Not to mention what's going on! This helps to keep the pace of the game fast and exciting straight away, so you are hooked at the very start!

+1

LEVEL UP

You will usually continue training and learning throughout the game. At the start, you will usually face much easier enemies, puzzles and traps than you will at the end. This is called a 'learning curve'. The more you play, the better you become at the basic skills meaning you will easily defeat low-level villains. So, the game starts to get harder the more you play. This keeps it challenging – and people who love action-adventure games love a challenge! If the games didn't do this, you'd quickly get bored. If the game gets too difficult too quickly, you get frustrated that you can't make any progress. Games are carefully designed to make the most of this.

COLLECTIBLES AND ACCESSORIES

Many games will have things that you can collect, scattered along your path through the story. These could be anything, from things that exist in the game world, such a little treasures, artworks or landmarks, to more *abstract* items such as playing cards or symbolic items such as skulls. There can also be items such voice recordings, diary entries, letters and photos which will help explain the story or give more information about characters, locations or events. These can have an active effect on the story, open new options in the gameplay, or simply be something you collect for fun. Some people like to play until they have found every single item, while others prefer to stick to the main game and don't bother searching too far off the beaten path. Usually, it is up to you which you choose.

CUTSCENES

At important moments throughout the game's story, the gameplay will stop and a short scene will be shown.

MOCAP

MOTION CAPTURE

Everyone loves a *pixelated* plumber, but characters in video games have come a long way. Many action-adventure games have brilliant stories and really interesting characters, so modern graphics have to be very realistic. More and more, actors and voice artists are bringing characters to life. One of the ways that game designers make characters move realistically is motion capture – known as mocap.

MoCap technology can be very expensive – but as stories in video games become more and more important, and video games compete with movies for people's attention and time, this technique means that fight scenes, conversations and characters can look very realistic.

In optical motion capture, the actor wears a special suit, which is covered in little sensors. Sometimes these sensors are also stuck on the actor's face. Special cameras record the actors' performance, and a computer uses the information from these cameras to create a digital 'skeleton' of the actor in a software program. The points on the body where sensors are placed can then be mapped to the same points on the animated character. The animation will then move exactly how the actor did.

ACTOR

↓

MAPPED POINTS

↓

SKELETON

↓

CHARACTER

CONSOLE PROFILE

Sony's PlayStation brand is one of the most successful gaming consoles ever. Let's take a look at the console that changed the game.

1994: PLAYSTATION

Data: The first of this notable series of consoles was the first console ever to sell 120 million units. The PlayStation was also the first to use rounded controllers, and had 3D graphics and the now iconic buttons. Slimline versions were released under the name PSONE.

THE DUALSHOCK CONTROLLER

Data: PlayStation's third controller design featured something new: the controller vibrated in time with events in the game. More modern versions also use lights and have a speaker.

2013: PLAYSTATION 4

Data: The PlayStation 4 sold 1 million units on its first day of release, and was the fastest-selling console in history. It later featured an add-on peripheral in the form of PlayStation VR – a virtual reality headset connected to the PS4. The PS4 was also released in a slim version and a pro version. The Pro version has a faster *processor* which creates very high-definition graphics.

2000: PLAYSTATION 2

Data: The PlayStation 2 is the most successful gaming console in the world. It sold over 155 million units and featured many blockbuster games, including Gran Turismo, Tekken and Tomb Raider. Slim and Super Slim versions were later released.

2005: PLAYSTATION PORTABLE

Data: The PSP, as it was known, was the first handheld PlayStation console. As well as playing games, it could connect to your console, browse the internet, and play TV programmes.

2011: PLAYSTATION VITA

Data: The PlayStation Vita was designed to appeal to mobile gamers, and looked similar to the PSP. It had a new feature called Remote Play, which meant that gamers with a PSN account could play their PS4 games on the handheld console too.

2006: PLAYSTATION 3

Data: The PS3 was the first home console that could play **Blu-ray** discs. It was also the console to launch the PlayStation Network (PSN) – PlayStation's online gaming service. The PlayStation Portable and the PlayStation Vita could also connect to the PS3.

FACT FILE: ŌKAMI HD

One of the most influential action-adventure games of all time is Okami. In terms of gameplay it was loosely inspired by The Legend of Zelda, but the story is more directly drawn from Japanese mythology.

Okami is a great example of a game where restrictions placed on its design resulted in genre-defining innovation. The game, created by a now-closed developer called Clover Studio, was one of the last games to appear on Sony's PlayStation 2 before the company moved on to its successor, the PS3. The relatively underpowered PS2 console forced the developers to abandon more realistic visuals in favour of a *cel-shaded* art style. It was actually a perfect fit and suited a style of artistic design that looked just like classic Japanese watercolour paintings.

This simpler art style not only looked beautiful but it also allowed the developers to use the power of the console in other areas, notably in the Celestial Brush, which along with the art style defined the game. The mechanic is used across all areas of the game, including combat, puzzle-solving, and during general exploration, with players using the brush to interact with the screen in interesting ways.

During this beautiful and captivating tale, players take on the role of a god called Amaterasu, who takes the form of a white wolf to save the land from darkness. This game has been re-released on each subsequent console generation because of its beautifully appealing gameplay. Okami HD is the most recently updated version and is available on PC, PS4, Switch and Xbox One. The very best video games are works of art, and Okami stands next to games like Shadow of the Colossus as a timeless experience that has been enjoyed by players on every console generation since its initial release.

MUSIC MAKES THE VIRTUAL WORLD GO ROUND

Because many action-adventure games have such dramatic storylines, creating the right atmosphere for the unfolding drama is very important. Game designers use all sorts of tricks to achieve this, but one of the most interesting is the way they use music.

CHIP TUNES

Early video games (or modern-day *retro* games) used simple, plinky-plonky tunes in their games. These tunes have a very distinctive, electronic sound, and are known as chip tunes because the sounds were generated by a computer chip. As they are often very repetitive, the tunes quickly become instantly recognisable as part of a particular game – some musicians even used them in real-world music.

ADAPTIVE MUSIC & SOUNDTRACK

Have you ever noticed how, when you're watching a movie, the music seems to change as the mood of the movie does? The dun-dun-DUNN at the scary part, the smooth violins at the mushy bits, the faster beats in the car chases? This type of music is put there on purpose to get the audience to feel what the director wants them to feel. Well, it's the same with video games. Certain types of music are chosen for certain parts of the game. For example, if you move from a safe area to a dangerous area the music will change. But video games have a much harder job to do when it comes to getting the music to *enhance* the mood and setting, and not distract from it. In a movie, the action will always happen in the same order, at the same exact times. *Composers* can then watch the movie and write one piece of music for it. But in games, lots of things can happen to make you take a different path through the game, and at different speeds. So, composers have to create something called adaptive music. Composers create 'blocks' of music that they can put together in lots of different orders. This means that the blocks can change easily into any mood as quickly as the player changes areas.

MUSICAL CUES

It's worth paying attention to the music; it can tell you a lot. Did it suddenly speed up? Better get running! Did the music suddenly go quiet? Step carefully and keep your wits about you. Adaptive music will work with you – so if you head down a corridor full of enemies, you'll hear the music change. But if you turn around and leave, it might change back again, letting you know you are safe. Keep your ears switched on, it might just save you a life or two!

FACT FILE: The Last Guardian™

When it comes to releasing a game, there's a set pattern that most titles follow. A studio will start work on a game when they have a good idea and the money to make it. Eventually, when it's ready to for people to see it, the publisher and developer will announce it. They'll show it off to the press and they'll make trailers, it'll appear at some public shows like Gamescom and E3, and then it'll release either on the date the publisher originally announced, or a while after if there's a hold up.

That's not what happened with The Last Guardian, though. This game, an action-adventure game by Team ICO for PlayStation, first went into development all the way back in 2007, when the PlayStation 2 was in its prime. Team ICO had made a game called Shadow of the Colossus, and this game was really well-loved, so everyone was very excited when they announced the follow-up in the summer of 2009… Fans rejoiced, and waited…

Both the PS2 and the PS3 came and went, and so it wasn't until 2015 that the game was announced – to rapturous applause – at games show E3. This time, the game was bound for Sony's new console, the PlayStation 4. Eventually, The Last Guardian launched in December 2016, and fans were finally able to get their hands on one of the most anticipated games of all time.

After countless hours of hard work and some undoubtedly frustrating setbacks, Team ICO delivered an emotional and engaging game about a boy and his giant, gryphon-like companion, Trico. In a strange and mystical land, a young boy discovers a mysterious creature, with which he forms a deep, unbreakable bond. The unlikely pair must rely on each other as they journey through ruins, facing unknown dangers. This is a beautiful game with an extraordinary story – and all of its fans agree, it was well worth the wait.

CONTINUE?

Yes, we made it! Well done, adventurer! OK: time to go and grab the treasure. Are you coming? Or would you like to stay here in the Arcade and learn some more...?

<<CONTINUE? Y/N>>
HTTPS://WWW.LEGO.COM/EN-GB/
GAMES/VIDEOGAMES

<<CONTINUE? Y/N>>
HTTPS://WWW.PLAYSTATION.COM/EN-
GB/GAMES/THE-LAST-GUARDIAN-PS4/

<<CONTINUE? Y/N>>
HTTP://WWW.DIGITALSCHOOLHOUSE.ORG.UK/

<<CONTINUE? Y/N>>
HTTPS://WWW.OKAMI-GAME.COM/

GLOSSARY

abstract	something not relating to a specific reality
AI	artificial intelligence; a computer simulation of human intelligence
Blu-ray	a disc format that is capable of storing 4k graphics and Dolby TrueHD audio
boss fights	the biggest and hardest battle of a particular level or game
cel-shaded	a non-realistic style of art used in video games and animation that has a cartoon-like, hand-drawn appearance
combat	physical and often violent battles
composers	people who write music
decade	a block of ten years
diverse	a wide range of people, places, or things
electronic	powered by electricity; usually a machine
enhance	to make better or more immersive
fetch quests	missions where a desired object must be collected and then returned
first-person	seeing through the eyes of a character as if you are them
franchises	lots of brands owned by one company
genre	a particular type or sort of something
iconic	well known and recognised around the world
objective	the main goal or target
parkour	free running, usually over, on or around large objects
persevere	continue to try
phenomenon	a remarkable event or trend
pixel	tiny dots of light that make up the images on a screen
pixelated	an image divided into small squares, rather than being smooth and clear
platform	a type of electronic device
processor	the part of a computer that handles tasks
retro	something made in the same style or fashion of something much older
side quests	optional missions that aren't part of the main storyline
top-down	a video game where the player looks at the action from above
toys-to-life	a video game feature using physical action figures to interact within the game

<<SAVING KNOWLEDGE. DO NOT SHUT DOWN. SYSTEMS SHOW GOOD KNOWLEDGE RETENTION. WELL DONE.>>

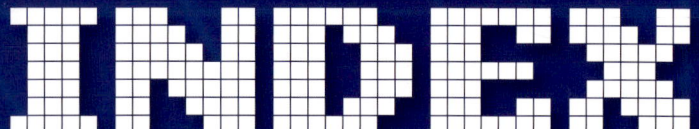

INDEX

<<THANKS FOR ACCESSING THE ARCADE TODAY. WE HOPE YOU HAD A PLEASANT TIME. SHUTTING DOWN IN 3... 2... 1...>>